safe
passage

safe
passage

Words to Help the Grieving

MOLLY FUMIA

CONARI PRESS

Published in 2003 by Conari Press,
an imprint of Red Wheel/Weiser, LLC
York Beach, ME
With offices at:
368 Congress Street
Boston, MA 02210
www.redwheelweiser.com

Library of Congress Cataloging-in-Publication Data
Fumia, Molly.
      Safe passage: words to help the grieving / by Molly Fumia.
          p. cm.
      ISBN 1-57324-901-7
      1. Grief. 2. Bereavement—Psychological aspects. I. Title.
BF575.G7F86 1992
155.9'37—dc20   92-10253

Interior design by Suzanne Albertson
Typeset in Perpetua
Printed in Canada
TCP
10 09 08 07 06 05 04 03
 8 7 6 5 4 3 2 1

In memory of
Bob Brown,
Evelyn and Margarita Tommy,
and Aaron Martin

Acknowledgments

I would like to reconfirm and multiply my love and gratitude to the marvelous support group who, over the years, have made the heart of this book possible. Luckily for me, I am in debt to the following people:

Chuck, Melissa, Mark, Nicholas, Gino, Kristen and Joel Fumia, John and Rena Fumia, Bob Brown, Tom Gumbleton, Debbie Fumia, Nancy Ottoboni, Debbie Biondolillo, Chris Hayes, Kathy Gibson, Cathy Wilcox, Terry Johnston, Ph.D., and Elie Wiesel.

To the late Helen Menden and Joe Biondolillo.

To the first brave hearts: Ann Morrissey and Carol Matusich.

And to the second wave of seers, supporters, and grief companions in my life: Sue Eschelbach, Al and Kathy Zapala, Marilyn and Bob Dumesnil, Bill Muller, S.J., Kathy Imwalle, Sharon Wulf, Nancy Holleran, Jennifer Pearson, Daisy Anzoategui, Barbara Ferst, David Ferst, Suzanne Sattler, IHM, and Jean Stokan.

To these extraordinary women—Judy Peckler, Jane Nakatani, Maria Dammer, Sydney Brown, and Glenda

Martin—I offer nothing less than wonder and amazement. You are the presence, and the proof, of energy capable of conquering grief. Because you are in my life, I dance a daily jig of delight.

And again, to Mary Jane Ryan, the Wise and Loving, all the thanks I can give.

Contents

Introduction

You might want to simply open this book to
any page and begin.

Or, you might want to start here . . .

This is a book of meditations for the grieving. A friend once said that writing it was
a brave thing. But I knew the braver thing
would be to read it.

It is true that grief is a journey, often perilous and
without clear direction, one that demands to be taken.
Sometimes, it begins quietly. Your reaction to shocking
news is measured, like a tossed stone in a placid lake,
circles of meaning slowing widening, reaching into more
and more of your consciousness until you understand
how much you have lost and grief washes over you.

But more often, grief begins cruelly—a few words,
the sharp suspension of reality. A moment of disbelief
and then the hailstorm descends, feelings like knives
slicing through bone, a relentless attack that will continue

into undefined time. Denial, fear, despair, anger, powerlessness, regret, guilt, loneliness—any or all of these feelings batter you mercilessly, causing you to doubt a way out of your pain.

To whatever degree you grieve, the emotional invasion is inevitable; the feelings are valid and real. This book is an attempt to put words around your feelings— something like facing the enemy. You can fight them, or you can live through them.

The very act of struggling to breathe when grief has deprived you of air is a sign of your spirit stirring. Even as the heart is breaking, the pieces begin to inch back. Even though the little things bring sobs up to your throat, and confusion has crushed any sense of normalcy in your life, something within you is plotting survival.

I offer these meditations as one map of your journey through the blackest night to the slow, gentle dawn of acceptance, unexpected wisdom, and new possibilities.

If you would, allow me to start at my own beginning. The first step to healing is to be brave enough to actually feel. For me, that prospect was terrifying. So I pushed the feelings aside for a long time. What I didn't know is that grief can be postponed, but it will not be denied.

Thirty years ago, our firstborn son, Jeremy, died in infancy. I was young and in shock. I was given bad counsel—don't put yourself through it, there is nothing you can do. My husband and members of our families went to see him. Everyone said goodbye except me.

I did not grieve for him; at least, not then. Not when we buried him, along with all of our hopes and dreams for a love that would outlive us rather than disappear into the empty space where Jeremy should have been.

Ten years later, after four more children, after a decade's worth of life and blessed wisdom, the dark chamber of my emotions where I had carefully stored my grief burst open. My anguish over the death of my son had stayed with me, waiting for me to call it forth. And when I did, I found myself overcome with sadness so painful, regret so harsh, guilt so penetrating, I knew that the feelings had compounded themselves into a powerful force that now controlled me, demanding that I pay the vast debt of my denial beginning immediately, without debate, without mercy.

Yet still the healing began and brought revelations. I learned that grief is the most patient and persistent of life companions. We all grieve. Being alive requires of us a relationship with the mysterious, life-long experience of letting go, whether it be the small daily dyings that mark our existence, or the gripping, transformative experience of finally saying farewell to someone we have loved.

I realized that grief is an ancient, certain link between all those who have ever mourned. My experience mirrored that of others, and I was comforted. And then I was empowered, immersed in the connectedness of all human suffering. I considered the causes of grief in a world drowning in sorrow.

The sources of grief are as varied as the grief-stricken. Spouses and partners, parents and children, beloved friends and compassionate onlookers—no one is spared the shattering loss of a loved one from old age and accidents, a legion of cancers, heart disease, AIDS, alcoholism, starvation, neglect, quirks of fate. . .

As we grieve, so does the world. We are confronted with death by inhumanity in every new headline. Violence, hatred, greed, ignorance, revenge, senseless disregard for human life—the dead seem to blend together in a common grave while the bereaved cling to a solitary, deeply personal memory. Blessed are those who peer into the images of devastation and define the faces of both the lost and the left behind.

Clearly, it is human connection that fuels the movement through grief. I know something about how you feel, as you do about me, and we are somehow changed. We find ourselves living in a larger world, sharing in the real sufferings of our time. And from that joining, we are also destined to share in the real joys now hidden, as yet unimagined, awaiting us as we emerge from our time of mourning.

Every corner of the world is a stage for the new possibilities offered by the sharing of grief. As one example, I offer a story from one of my trips to El Salvador. I found there what many others have found: a living, breathing, collective memory; a source of power arising from the graves of thousands, now inhabiting the spirits of the survivors; a courageous, wonderfully loving people.

The Salvadorans call the mysterious marriage of suffering and hope *mistica*. "Mistica is as ordinary as sacrifice for others," says Renny Golden in *The Hour of the Poor, the Hour of Women*, "and as inexplicable as the appearance of insurgent hope in those moments when Western psychologists would predict despair or paralyzing grief."

Mistica comes alive in the story of Rufina Amaya Marques, the only survivor of the massacre, in December 1992, of 1000 women, men, and children in the town of El Mozote. From her hiding place in the grass, Rufina heard her four children cry out to her just before they were brutally slain by members of the Salvadoran military. For a year, Rufina wandered the countryside, her despair and guilt leaving her barely coherent.

Today, Rufina works at a day care center. She told us that she survived because the people around her never left her to grieve alone. They did not suggest that she forget, nor did they abandon her in all her years of sadness. They celebrated with her each sign of healing.

Rufina's devastating sorrow and subsequent resurrection has broken the boundaries of any single event. "I cannot allow hatred to kill me, too," she says. "If I give in to hatred, I will become like the murderers. Instead I give in to love, and the children I lost continue. In the end, love will be victorious." In the case of Rufina Amaya, her grief, shared with that of an entire nation, now insists that the future must be different.

I believe that what sustains Rufina is an everyday miracle. Love paves the way for what begins as a solo journey and becomes a pilgrimage of many. People will want to accompany you—you might consider inviting them along. Let them love you. What transforms our mutual grieving into "insurgent hope" is our recognition that to suffer and to love is what we do together, for each other, in honor of each other.

No matter what lies in the future for you, I wish first to honor the unique experience of your grief. I hope to offer a hand to steady you on your journey. My words are both a record of experiences and my own interpretation of the feelings that might first haunt, then inhabit, and finally restore your spirit. The reflections are collected under six "signposts" to light your way.

The reflections in "Beginnings" and "Navigation" consider the harsh beginnings of grieving. I hope that you will find your feelings in these words and return to any that have meaning for you at the moment.

At a time when you want only to reverse time and recreate events, life will move you on. In "Surrender" and "Transformation," I have tried to give voice to new emotions. Some suggest a sense of forward motion or renewed energy, or celebrate a stronger step and a day without weeping. This is the part of the journey where you might be less afraid of memories and more inclined to imagine feeling differently.

The final meditations are contained in "Continuance" and "Connection." Respecting your immersion into complex emotions, your resurfacing to hope, your awareness of those who stand beside you, whether intimate friends or unnamed companions, I suggest that at least one destination for the road you have traveled is in the wider universe.

In the end, grief cannot be ordered. Elements of every part of the journey dwell under every signpost along the way. It is a start and stop, forward and back, inside and out process that, if we dare enter it, will eventually leave us sadly experienced, profoundly affected, and deeply changed. Just like love, it is both a dreaded and miraculous event.

BEGINNINGS

"*Consolation springs from sources
deeper far than deepest suffering.*"

—WILLIAM WORDSWORTH

alking by the sea, I pick up a starfish that is missing an arm. Losing you has been like that, like a limb actually was torn from my body.

As I gently place it back on the sand, I notice that despite the cruel amputation, a marvelous and beautiful creature has survived. And I remember the miracle of the starfish: the arm will grow back, and it will be whole once again.

There is an instant between awakening and awareness that I float free of remembrance and reality. For only a moment, things are as they were, and this present pain is not at all. I wish not to move on, but to stay safe in that nothingness, to linger, while I can, just ahead of the dreaded truth.

The center of my grief is like the dead of winter; the white, frozen stillness surrounds me, a deep, interior chill pervades my body. I am terrified that I will always be this cold.

The slight warming wind that will unsettle the ice is not yet perceptible.

I cry and I cry. I respond to every turn of the day with tears, wondering, now and then, how my incessant weeping appears to those around me. It is coming clear to me. Only tears encourage time to pass. Only tears anoint the endless waiting with tender hope that the days to follow might flow more kindly into understanding.

I am so tired. These callous circumstances have stolen away my energy and my motivation. I am left without the power to continue moving; I can hardly imagine the strength even to stand in place.

I want only to give in to my exhaustion, to sleep and sleep until I can wake up to another, less evil reality.

What is it like, this place set aside for grieving? It is wherever we are surrounded by the darkness. And where does the healing begin? Huddled in the dark, listening to long-lost voices, not yet searching for the light.

I wake, haunted by a searing sense of the unfinished. By how things might have been. If only I possessed the magic power to give us a second chance. But I am no wizard; the trick I must perform is to accept what is.

This pain is a companion, but can it ever become something more? The answer is in my ability to befriend my own experience.

"*I*n dealing with fear, the way out is in."

—SHELDON KOPP

Grief is not passive, but active. Grief reveals and challenges while it deals with the horrible facts. It lends itself to truth in a way that no other emotion can. It identifies all of the participants in tragedy and allows them their role in the universe.

And in all of this, I now somehow take my place.

*W*e struggled so hard to be together, and now we are apart once more. I can't imagine starting over with someone else. You were my last destination.

A kaleidoscope of feelings has ensnared me. Denial, anger, guilt, despair, acceptance. One does not end for another to begin, rather the emotions tumble about and crash together just beyond control, and without regard for my wounded, weeping heart.

I am waiting to become disentangled. I want to separate one color from another, so that I might see more clearly what assaults me. I want to address the fullness of my tears one feeling at a time.

They tell me to take it easy, give yourself time, just sit for a while. But that doesn't work. They tell me to keep busy, go on a trip, take up something new. That doesn't work either. To do nothing, to do everything. Nothing works. Nothing works.

Mourning is like re-entering the womb. We find a dark place where we can weep unheeded and become whole in our own time. Emptiness turns to hope in this safe refuge, this comforting cavern echoing endings and beginnings, slowly transformed again into a passageway to our other, older life.

I was shocked that I did not die from grief. And I know now that I will not die from it, because I choose not to. I may run, or shake wildly, or lie paralyzed on the ground for a while, but I will not ultimately succumb.

I find myself going over and over the details of your death with everyone I know. To speak and speak again of this event proclaims its awful truth to me, perhaps not yet quite convinced, perhaps not sure of my place in its unfolding.

And so I allow this repetition, knowing that words are possibilities—of explanation, of comprehension, of absolution. My testimony, once familiar, will reassure my trembling, still questioning heart.

" **U**nderstanding does not cure evil, but it is a definite help, inasmuch as one can cope with a comprehensible darkness."

—CARL JUNG

*I*f only I could have spoken to him before he chose to end a life. It would only have taken a few minutes to tell him about us, to describe the ways we all love each other, to paint a picture of our happiness and our innocence.

I could have changed his mind. He would have understood that she deserved to live. I would have looked into his eyes and made him see himself in mine, and he would have decided differently.

*E*ven though I am surrounded by friends, I think about images of the past that are still present for me.

Which of these ghosts, if any, deserves my attention? It seems unkind to banish them all from among the living, from a place that was once theirs.

But I want to laugh again, to participate once more in lively conversation. While I welcome those memories that have been invited, I will eventually close the door on those which haunt me.

I haven't eaten in days. Eventually, I'll have to eat. When I feel like eating again, I hope I won't feel guilty, but will respect my sense that it is all right for me to live, even though you have died.

Running from my grief, I am not silent or still long enough to let it in. But the fullness of existence is facing both life and death, and taking the risks involved in that confrontation.

To have loved you is to have opened up to a willingness to feel your loss. This is the time of reckoning. I must stop to feel my sorrow.

How are you how are you how are you. Fine fine fine.

Not fine. . . . Terrible.

She tells me to call and we'll have lunch or go shopping. She says I have to do something, but those aren't the things I want to do.

I know what I want to do. I want to cry and cry shamelessly and I want her to hold me while I'm doing it.

Grief is a trail of dreams, fulfilled and unfulfilled, all that could have been, never can be again. On this forlorn night walk, the path to new promises is still beyond the horizon, awaiting the hazy, yet inevitable, future.

I am disoriented by death. I do not know where I have been or where I am going. The familiar landmarks are out of view, coldly covered by death's icy grip.

My confusion has, at least, demanded that I cease moving. Standing still will restore my sense of direction, and what remains of my inner fire will warm the way toward healing.

I am afraid to be angry. Rage betrays the need to accept what has happened. Yet I am also afraid to accept. Acquiescence might suggest that I have given in to fate and to the injustice of your being taken from me.

Despite the taboo on anger, I sense that I have that right, even though fury will not alter the facts. It is not, "I understand, but I am furious." It is, "I understand *and* I'm furious."

For now, to survive, I choose both acceptance and indignation. Then even though your loss will never be okay, someday I will be.

We need a grieving room for all of us who are mourning, a quiet, safe place of solace where emotion is sacred and the continual falling of tears generates the energy for our healing.

We need a grieving room with thick walls to keep despair outside and hope secure within, and, on the floor, comfortable pillows to remind us to rest.

" ife is a tragic mystery. We are pierced and
driven by laws we only half understand . . .
we find that the lesson we learn again and again is
that of accepting heroic helplessness."

—FLORIDA SCOTT-MAXWELL

A friend of mine suggested that when I feel lost and don't know what to do next, I should quiet myself with the question, "What is needed now?" The answer will not only be a first step out of my present confusion, but a lasting gift to myself.

*T*he incredible pain of some ritual of the daily. . . .

Your clothes came back from the cleaners. Your dentist appointment is still tacked onto the refrigerator. The spaces in my calendar are full not only of the things we have done, but the things we still have to do. How could I have been so fooled? When I noted each event on the page, I had thought its certainty to be assured.

As I touch again and again the still-warm body of the life we had, I torture myself with longing for the ordinary. I am trying to endure each pain patiently; despite the shards of simple things, I sense that a new, more gracious reality might await me.

Sleeping, which used to relieve the fullness of the day, has become just another difficult task.

I first avoid my bed, knowing that if I stop moving, memories will sneak into my fading consciousness and force a sob up into my throat.

Other nights I lie awake for hours—feeling nothing, but still unable to capture sleep. Or I wake in the predawn darkness, hoping desperately that the clock has moved toward morning.

I was not prepared for sleep to be an enemy. What I need now is a friend, and a way to rest my weary spirit.

*L*ong ago we were taught to ignore grief rather than enter into it. Simply to hang on mindlessly until it is over.

But this old precept cannot bear the weight of profound experience. Neat categories cannot accommodate the muddle of mature emotion. To get through grief, we let go rather than hang on, watching for the inner counselor who will guide us, ever mindful of the process that will slowly, patiently lead us where we need to go.

Beginnings

What ever happened to happily ever after? As it turns out, that was the cruelest part of the fairy tale.

"Hope is hearing the melody of the future;
faith is dancing to it today."

—RUBEN A. ALVEZ

I lie around with nowhere to go, like a
crumpled, discarded coat. The pursuits of
the past fail to interest me in the bitter present. All
the color has gone out of the world; life has been
redone in grays, dull and uninviting.

But while today it seems appropriate to give in
to mourning, I notice the slowly widening pastel of
the horizon. This sorrow will not be forever. I will
have somewhere to go again, and new interests to
draw me there.

All in good time, they say. And even now, while
time stands stubbornly still, I know that it is true.

I will not blame God or destiny for my loss. Instead I will ask God to weep with me and encourage destiny to favor me with another hand.

*I*solation is the worst case scenario of grieving. They say that my pain begs to be shared; yet I seem to be pulling away, separating from everyone. Only by avoiding feelings can I come close to another. Only by avoiding others can I bear to feel.

The way back to intimacy requires crossing a killing field of emotion. I will risk it eventually, and perhaps those who wait for me on the other side will find returning to them a less fearful, more trusting spirit.

" *I* hear a voice within me telling me to stop mourning the past. I too want to sing of love and of its magic. I too want to celebrate the sun, and the dawn that heralds the sun."

—ELIE WIESEL

The loss of someone we love is an imprisonment. We give over our freedom and lock ourselves up inside, with nothing to do but dwell on the event that has condemned us.

This confinement will not last; the weapons of the human spirit, reflection and imagination, will eventually demand our release. Our yearning for the old life will yield to our imagining of the new, and the anguish that has so bound us will gently fall away.

You are my enemy; my rage is unending. I know it is unhealthy. But I can't stop wanting to find you and tie you down and spend days telling you what you took away from me. I would pummel you with the truth until you wept. And then I would open up and drench you with the rest of my feelings, until you were drowning in regret.

Just when you were screaming for air, I would let you go. I would watch you crawl away. If I have to live in the aftermath of what you've done, so must you.

The something that is not lost, even when the other person is gone, is the self. This may be an ending, but it is not the end.

Trust pain as well as comfort, perhaps more. For in pain we notice everything; in comfort there is not need to be alert.

Believe, therefore, in your pain. Be present to it. Own it. The most deeply felt discomfort will not obscure your vision of redemption but clarify it, until it is fitting to be comfortable again.

Getting through the day is like walking through a mine field of deadly moments of recollection.

Just when I have slipped beneath the surface of remembering, drawn there by the benevolent distractions of daily life, the grim new reality suddenly explodes around me, reminding me that everything is terribly, permanently different. And I must absorb the same first brutal shock, the same descending horror, over and over again.

I am deceived by those instances of forgetfulness, yet I am obviously not ready to live every moment with the inalterable truth.

In the absence of explanation, of understanding, of meaning, I find myself returning to the simple truths of childhood.

And just as I did as a child, I will slip my hand into God's hand for that familiar feeling of comfort and reassurance.

I lie in the dark, aware that in the distance, the music of life is playing. Even in my grieving for you, I am drawn to the sounds and my body begins to stir.

Your voice, next to me in the night, gives me a little nudge. "Go ahead. Dance."

So I stand up, still clothed in darkness, and hold up my arms. A long twirl, a low dip. Silently, I come to life like a marionette who has been touched by magic.

Please don't give me away—not yet. I'm not ready for anyone else to know I'm dancing in the darkness.

id you wait to leave me until you felt me let you go? I didn't want to, you know, and would have fought forever had it not been for your eyes. "It's okay," they said to me, clear and certain, even as they began to close.

Thank you for giving me that. I know you would have preferred to stay; I was ready to hold you here. But we decided that a lifetime of relationship was more worthy of a long, knowing embrace than a bewildered, bitter parting. We could not fear too greatly for the end of love when we are the proof of its continuation.

*I*n recent, endless days, feelings have overtaken me, until I know the very in and out of my breathing would cease without the energy of emotion. Long ago I would have doubted my chances for survival in this explosive state. But I have learned to trust the resilience of my own spirit, that place of power from which feelings come. I have learned to look for healing in the logic of the heart.

NAVIGATION

"Your pain is the breaking of the shell that
encloses your understanding. Even as the stone of
the fruit must break, that its heart may stand
in the sun, so must you know pain."

—KAHLIL GIBRAN

I begin at the beginning, examining each frame of memory. Images of another time rage in my stormy awareness, and I am jolted with searing sprays of inexorable change.

As hurt washes over me, I am tempted to abandon this cruel immersion. But I stay here, shivering, clinging to comprehension that is still raw, believing that my very presence in these cold waters of remembrance will soon turn them warm and soothing.

I am fighting a cauldron of feelings that stir violently within me. Emotion is, indeed, my enemy. It keeps everything from returning to the way it was. Easy and unexamined. The way I planned it.

And yet, I am tempted to give in. My emotions are too large, and the plan has all but disappeared. If I come to know this enemy, perhaps I will find in the very pouring out of feelings a better friend than the delusion of control.

You are gone and my grief, as was our love, is not really public. It was a decision we made to keep us safe, we said, from some of those who love us, and all of those who don't.

But the grief I feel for you is large, and loud, and threatening to burst out of me and paint everything the colors of who we were. Know that I would do that for you, make posters and take out ads telling everyone about our gorgeous, great love. Give me a sign, my beloved, and I will do it.

I am imprisoned in a cell of loneliness. There is no way out, except for the unexpected touch of others. Their affection will guide me down the passageway to my freedom. Their encouragement will illuminate the way.

I lie awake at night, tortured by a barrage of questions that pick at my flesh like tiny birds with sharp beaks:

Why me? Why now? What have I done to deserve this? What could I have done to prevent this cruel parting?

Unanswerable questions. All I can do is let them flow through me, rather that pick raw my tender skin. Oh yes, here they are again, my night visitors.

We need to honor the truth of our experience, whatever it is—anger at the person who died, rage at God, guilt at being alive. Surveying the horizon of our emotions lets us know how and where we are wounded.

We gather inside a building to celebrate life in spite of death. I welcome the transformation: a door has become a passageway to hope, mere walls, a fortress of faith.

But even as I seek the comfort and familiarity of this holy place, my voice trembles as I continue with the prayers. I dread the return of our struggle, the eternal tension between God and humanity, between certainty and imagination, between believing and wanting to believe.

I wish my spirit were as solid as the structure that holds us here. Beyond my trembling, I know that ancient truths whisper again promises of consolation and peace.

" Perhaps if I had a coat of arms, This would be
  my motto:
  Weep and begin again."

—M.C. RICHARDS

I watch others from a distance moving effortlessly in the circle of family and I am angry that their lives still seem to be intact. I rage at the injustice of death, that anything can be undisturbed, that anyone can go on normally in the face of this event.

How is it the others haven't noticed that nothing will ever be the same again? I must be the only one who understands this small, yet eternal change.

I still recall being trapped in the Saturday matinee by a movie that turned out to be scary. Surrounded by small fidgeting bodies with cringing faces, afraid of the terrible images and of the foolishness of a sudden, knee-bumping departure, I simply closed my eyes.

Now it is grief who has trapped me, encircling me with your sweet memory, daring me to stay in my seat for a ragged newsreel of faded intimacies and forgotten celebrations.

I am no longer a child, but if simply closing my eyes could save me from my present fear, I would do it.

y spirit hurts, especially with the persistent feeling that you have forsaken me. I wonder at the exquisitely painful timing of your departure. Just when the future was unfolding rightly, you abandoned the plan; just when I counted on our togetherness, I find myself alone.

What happened to your promise of faithfulness and the sound of your voice echoing inside my own?

Refusing to feel will not change what has happened. But it is more than that: We must care for our feelings as if our lives depended upon them.

Emotional survival is to be found in our present grieving, because as surely as we are emptied by sorrow and loneliness, we will someday be filled with joy and desire. To be emotionally whole, our experience must be boundless, and our range of feelings complete.

When I find myself panicking, it's usually because I've let my mind wander off to the future—where will I be next year, how will I feel in two years, how will I survive Christmas and birthdays? An endless procession of empty days, weeks, months begin to line up in front of me like tombstones waiting to be inscribed with memories never made.

All I can do is bring myself back to today, to tomorrow maybe, and remember that the future is unknowable and my place in it is yet unborn.

I am engulfed with an emptiness that is thunderous. Time has become an echo: empty, empty. How will I ever fill up the moments? One at a time, one at a time.

For the grieving, that first, hesitant step into the rushing stream of feeling leaves us wondering why we ever left our comfortable little boat. But rest assured that when it is over, we will simply sail away again.

I feel a magnitude of sadness that is no more than infinite, and I am inconsolable. I see that death is no respecter of persons, and I am without hope.

But when I am tempted to believe that what we lose is powerful enough to negate the ultimacy of love, every fiber of my being revolts. Whatever is left of my spirit will hold fast to love, until the invading forces of despair are finally turned away.

" *I* look at my own house and see the battle scars, the deep wounds and healing scabs. It's been a year splattered with scalding pain that allowed each of us to touch our core and see who and what we are. The house looks exhausted from the assaults and the slow healing process."

—SHERRY ARMENDARIZ

My anger at you for leaving me is scary. It goes against my idea of myself as a nice and reasonable person.

But you shouldn't have promised, by your mere existence, to always be here; you shouldn't have talked me into counting on you. What a cruel trick, to suggest an eternal relationship and then abandon our agreement. And to leave me alone to face fear, panic and finally, this terrible sadness, without you to hold me through it-some things may be unforgivable.

How could this be happening? As you can see, I am no longer nice nor reasonable. I am angry, but I suspect I'll never be so angry as to forget how I loved you.

The temptation is to allow death to claim more than its share, and leave us to our anger and powerlessness.

The challenge is to engage in life again with renewed energy, and embrace the new days with a gentle, welcoming spirit.

eath has separated us, but not completely. We have not parted company forever. I am only living away from you for a while.

s I continue grief's journey, my body aches
from its burden of overwhelming sorrow.
My throat is tight, my stomach knotted, my
chest bruised with an inner hurt that makes it
difficult to draw a breath. It feels as if my skin has
been removed and I am exposed to the brutality of
the world, undefended even by a thin protection.

I can only hope that as with other journeys,
there will be a time for rest. And as with other
hurts, my body will someday heal.

I am afraid I will get lost in the maze of my feelings, that I will go in there and never come out.

Still, I am unexplainably drawn into the dark labyrinth where I might find only despair and panic for companions. They will receive me there, and offer to take me through the darkness. If they plot the sole exit, I have no choice but to receive them too, befriend them in return for showing me the way.

I remember a time long ago when in anger, I wished you were dead. And now you are. It would be silly of me to claim responsibility for your fate, but some small childlike voice tempts me to do just that.

The truth is, I *did* want you to vanish at that now ancient moment. Not you, exactly, but the particular hurt you had become for me. Whatever loss of self I was experiencing, a sharp, personal slap in which you, indeed, had participated, led me to want to sweep both you and the pain away.

Luckily for you, wishes are not deeds, and my anger could not bring your end. Know that if wishes had more power, I would wish you right back to me. As it is, I am left with other memories, still close and real, of the deeds of love.

Healing is in our rage. It is in our confusion, our guilt, our remorse, our loneliness, in these things, not beyond them or outside of them. Acknowledging them will make them count toward change. Experiencing these feelings will mysteriously reveal healing's presence, and the new, softer energies that will direct the days to come.

" *E*verything precious including our dignity can be taken from us but the one thing that cannot be taken away is our power to choose what attitude we will take toward the events that have happened."

—VICTOR FRANKL

The depth of my grief is a constant with the breadth of my love. I would never sacrifice one to avoid the pain of the other.

When we are struggling through the night, falling prey to the beasts of guilt and regret, drowning in a river of tears, finally succumbing to exhaustion, we cannot be expected to believe in the beauty of the coming dawn. Somewhere in our past, we knew morning to be night's faithful follower, but for now, that understanding will have to force its way through the menacing darkness and back to us again.

The old should outlive the young. Between birth and death a life should unfold, creating and re-creating itself, given a chance to learn and grow, fail and succeed, love greatly and give birth to the next generation. We each are due our own time, safe between those who came before us and those who come after us. Any other way is unthinkable.

The emptiness is heavy, if that is possible. The loss of hope and dreams bears down on me. They say in time the burden will lift. But until then, my hollow self is alone with this stinging injustice. It should have been me.

*T*he season of grief is our shutting down time. We prepare the cottage of our hearts for the winter, securing our windows to the world, stocking the cupboards with what will sustain us during the cold and dark. Carefully we rebuild our inner fire, and huddle in its warmth while the storms of winter pass, awaiting a spring that will come as surely as the steady passage of the days.

S urely you remember me telling you, "Don't die without me."

The thought of being left here alone in the world always terrified me. I had thought we were going to do everything together.

And now you've left me here to do it by myself. I know you wouldn't have wanted it this way, and I forgive you your abandonment. But my need to see you and talk things over with you has not changed, even though everything else has.

So for now, I am alone. Yes, I know you would claim a new kind of togetherness, that somehow you are still with me. But I prefer the old way.

ome of my friends are uncomfortable with death. I don't blame them, because we work hard to keep death hidden away. Despite the fact that dying is happening all of the time, we choose to believe it isn't there.

Yet only with familiarity comes understanding. I have been brought close to dying by someone I love, and we are getting acquainted, death and I. I will never be as afraid as I used to be.

Giving death a place in my life is healthy for my living.

We know ourselves by the stories we tell.

Losing you has dismantled my storyline and shaken my plot; the tale I tell about who I am and where I am going doesn't make sense anymore.

I want desperately to find other words that will imagine my life anew. I just don't know where and how that story will begin.

"Grief is a very antisocial state."

—PENELOPE MORTIMER

Even though I am encircled by friends, I wonder when my loneliness will cease. Even though I am surrounded by the familiar, I wonder if l will ever feel at home again. I am alone and lost, and I am enraged that I could have been so cruelly sent far away from what used to comfort me.

*I*f I could tell you my one regret, it would be that I didn't love you better. I had always intended to improve upon that, because you deserved to be well loved.

And if you could tell me your one regret, it would be that everyone deserves to be well loved. With that in mind, I will lend the world whatever energy for love I still possess, and improve upon things in your name.

rieving is an invitation to what we believe to be divine. We will find in this hallowed meeting the blessing of our every emotion and the grace to believe in the mystical power of whatever we are feeling.

It is the small things that bring me to incredible sorrow. I come across a photo in a drawer, and I have to step back in order to avoid being engulfed by your absence. Confronted with the problem of your clothes in the closet, I know that taking them away will not be possible without dying once more.

The message is unmistakable: I must give myself good time, because the little things are not little at all.

My mind is caught in the tangled threads of grudge and passion, but my heart is freed by the strong bonds of acceptance and love.

Grief is about unfinished business. All that still aches to be done, said, or felt together. Although our plan, fading quickly, is surrendered, something continues: a connection not based on the future and an understanding that is simply present as I resume the journey alone.

"Do not fear the truth,
hard as it may appear,
grievously as it may hurt,
it is still right
and you were born for it.
If you go out to meet
and love it,
let it exercise your mind,
it is your best friend
and closest sister."

—DOM HELDER CAMARA,
The Desert is Fertile

rieving takes longer than we want it to. Days, months, even years go by and we discover that the shock waves still reverberate in our scarred spirits, that our grieving is still hesitant, still halting, still sparse of those occasions that are healing.

But grief runs by its own clock, and as surely as we sometimes mourn with agonizing slowness, we will leap through other days, making astonishing strides toward recovery.

Give voice to sorrow. Lend words to loneliness. Make heard the depth of your despair and the breaking of your heart.

For what remains unspoken can never burst into healing song.

Like a ritual I cannot abandon, I play again and again in my mind the scenes of our history. And at times, guilt ravages the heart, stills all hopefulness, and holds me hostage in a sad story with no ending.

But there is no way to re-create the past to make it come out differently. Our story must simply end without conclusion, and my story can begin again from there.

I am trapped, like a bird that has been caught in the house and is beating her wings frantically against the glass doors, wondering what is keeping her from the familiar freedom beyond.

Before I set about crashing through the glass, I stop to gather my strength. And in that moment of solitude, wings stilled, breath slowed, I turn to the interior of the room. I take only tiny steps, hopping noiselessly and carefully across unknown surfaces, making what I can of unexpected perches on the way up through the darkness. Until I finally feel the gentle ripple of open air against my body, and I slip out the hole in the roof to the sky.

After his death, there came a struggle between innocence and guilt, as if there were only two ways to explain the things that weren't quite right, and one must be chosen to complete the ordeal.

But in his dying he found freedom, and we survivors, too, are liberated. We can be merciful with ourselves and with those events that are now retired to memory. We, too, are entitled to the blessings of his transformation.

G rief wants not to be measured.

There is no scale which tips the way of the greatest loss, thus leaving a lesser sorrow to hang suspended and exposed in its smallness.

Our inclination to subject tragedy to comparison threatens recognition of the universal experience, and more importantly, our freedom to feel. The magnitude of our loss is irrelevant and ultimately incalculable.

" Self-pity in its early stages is as snug as a feather mattress. Only when it hardens does it become uncomfortable."

—MAYA ANGELOU

Dinner was our meeting place, a time for re-connection or for being silent, together. Then, a meal by myself once in a while seemed rather special. A good book or a good spot for gazing could spice up both the solitude and the food.

But solitude is so far from loneliness, and now, with you gone, eating alone seems sadly desolate and dangerously pointless. I will survive by grieving the loss of your companionship, and accepting the fact that this still necessary experience will be different, at least for awhile.

I first grieve by allowing you to take over my heart, struggling with your presence, sparring with the unspeakable idea that you are gone. My heart is occupied by memory and finality.

I next grieve by making room in that captive heart for myself. We must meet there one more time, you and I, to bind together in a common presence that is edgeless, endless. In that awareness, I can feel the uprising of an old ally. The self I still am continues, side by side in the universe, with the self you will always be, but insists I reclaim my heart as my own.

*I*f we avoid the grief of today, it will only pile up. Days and days of grieving, one upon the other, awaiting our attention.

Luckily, one can always find a place in the dark to begin again. And as the mountain of our mourning crumbles, the promise of a new, less burdened day will herald the dawn.

I am waiting to drown.

A crushing wave of sorrow has pulled me under with its powerful undercurrent of despair. After thrashing about, searching wildly for air, I have surrendered to the darkness.

Even while I wait, however, whatever remains of my consciousness senses hope. In the very waiting, I am soothed. In the very surrender, I might be healed.

There is someone inside of us who knows exactly what to do. Each of us possesses a natural wisdom that will guide us during this most difficult of times. By turning inward we will find our way through.

The curse of grieving is its bitter captivity,
the blessing to follow its sweet liberation.

I came across your handwriting on a piece of paper.

Cruelly I was yanked back to a single, carefree moment, set with childlike innocence in the middle of life and its activities. You didn't know what was ahead, nor did I. If only we could return to that instant of unknowing, when you were as alive as the movement of the pen on the page and as playful as the hand that held the pen, and linger there in the delight of the simple present.

This is not the end of joy.

    Grieving is bits of many things—memories, regrets, reminders—each of which bears its own special weight in our burden of sorrow. And each bit has to be gone through, patiently, silently, painfully, as one goes through old papers in a long-forgotten trunk, considering each one separately, remembering, assigning it to some new box within our hearts.

Healing, too, is bits of many things—smiles which multiply as the days pass; chilling remembrances turned warm by the returning sun; new loves. A day will come when there will be more bits of healing than of grieving, and reasons for joy will begin to pile up in the freshly swept rooms of our lives.

We cannot allow just one attitude to dominate us forever, especially unending melancholy, smoldering regret, or eternal penitence. Grieving calls forth all the stations of the self, to remind us of our complexity; any single facet of who we are cannot be solely sovereign over the spirit. We may be fragmented, but we are still complete.

" What 'disintegrates' in periods of rapid transformation is not the self, of course, but its defenses and ideas. . . . We do not need to protect ourselves from change, for our very nature is change."

—JOANNA MACY,
World as Lover, World as Self

Although sorrow enshrouds us like a coat that is too heavy and too large to easily shed, other things we used to be—joy, energy, interest in the world—are only a single layer away, lighter, more comfortable garments to wear as we are healing.

Surrendering to grief is like deciding to cross a river that we know has a rock bottom.

The first steps are nearly impossible; we hesitate on the shore, imagining that jagged edges will meet our tender feet. But the stones beneath us, though hard and cold, are also smooth.

We step slowly, feeling our way. Soon we are reaching for the stones, and for the mantel they lay through the murky waters.

SURRENDER

*"Life only demands from you the
strength you possess. Only one feat is
possible—not to have run away."*

—DAG HAMMARSKJOLD

I begin to wonder if it is I who died. Perhaps I'm even wishing for it, so as not to have these feelings.

But the life that still flows through me has watched my frantic flight from emotion and patiently awaits my return. The way I feel can never be the end of me.

Go where you will be healed, but take someone along who loves you, who will listen along the way, and with whom you can share a quiet toast when you reach your destination.

*I*n the beginning, memory is a night-stalker and imagination its cruel accomplice. Why, why? What if, what if?

Lying tangled and sweating in a nightmare of lost possibilities, we await the mercy of morning.

The dawn brings an unlikely companion: the past has become a friend. This is the surprise we have been waiting for. Suddenly, there is no struggle to hide from memory and imagination. Suddenly, memory is sweet and imagination liberating.

Recovery is marked by movement down and in, like diving beneath the surface of a stormy sea, to the stillness far below the torment. We find there an unanticipated reality, one that challenges the permanence and the potency of that which rages above. We find there a universe of quiet strength, of previously forbidden awareness.

ealing is not a wish that can be granted by someone else. It is a well within us that we alone can tap. It is a desire that we allow for, in our own time, by our own choosing.

Grief has left me feeling out of control.

A friend suggested that I center myself.
So I began the journey inward, and I found my
wounded heart still beating, and my aching lungs
still breathing in and out, slowing, quieting.

I was reminded of the life of which I am
still a part, not a small and limited existence that
begins and ends abruptly and coldly, but a warm,
expectant being, confident in the fullness of life.
And there, tucked in my center, I began to reclaim
my authority.

One marvels at the courage of the grieving, that they can eat a meal or enjoy a joke without stopping mid-bite or mid-laugh to weep instead.

"The dictionary defines *night* in terms of day and *day* in terms of night. Can we find a way to talk about light and dark without talking about good and bad? To love both day and night? Can we hold the beauty of both in the same breath?"

—RUTH GENDLER

on't let anyone talk you out of your grief. There will be those who urge you to move on, but that is not yet possible.

You cannot be persuaded to abandon something that you have become, as you have become this profound hurt. You are waiting, and they must wait with you. You will know when your identity is again changing, when the new person, who has lovingly layered her pain, her healing, and her new understanding around the skeleton of her soul, is ready to emerge.

What is the etiquette of mourning?

There isn't one. After all the attempts to comfort, the suggestions shared out of love and helplessness, each mourner says his own goodbyes, feels her own feelings, and moves uneasily and unevenly toward healing.

In the end, each struggling spirit, alone in the company of a few dear friends, somehow finds a way.

My sorrow has left me as defenseless as a lost child in a fairy tale, wandering about a great, dark forest, searching for something soothing and familiar. But as in fairy tales, there is a way out. It is the trail of discarded memories that I left as I walked that will eventually lead me home.

I marvel that I have not come apart. Yes, actually disintegrated. I imagine my molecules stretched to the limit, breaking up, and the bits of me simply floating away.

What has held me together? Has it been others who have kept the parts of me from straying? If that is so, I'm thankful for their attention, and quick hands, I suppose. But still I sense in myself some lurking power. Perhaps I'm better glued together than I thought.

Grief enters our lives and brings along unforeseen guides. Old friends and lost relations, listeners and interpreters, and once in a while, someone whose understanding is so surprising and so complete as to take one's breath away.

What do we know of the origin of this unexpected encounter? It is a messenger from the heavens. And what do we know of its destiny? It is a lasting presence.

*I*n grieving we face a sacred moment, one permeated with fear, overflowing with pain, steeped in difficulty.

Although we run from such an opportunity, its sacredness is in the sound of our returning footsteps.

"**I**s there anything I can do?"

Yes, you can turn back time, take away the hurt, and bring my loved one back.

And if that isn't possible, just be on my side while I face the demons.

Taking a daily measurement of our pain will reveal the surprising fact that it really can change. Even if, as yet, there is no day without pain, noticing the difference between excruciating agony and dull ache is important. The measure of change is a sign that there is actually a way out.

My friend: You do not say to me, "Cease grieving." Thank you. Until it is time to do so, I cannot stop this process, however strange and undesired it may be. But I promise you, your nearness now will help to bring my mourning to a gracious end.

"For something in you dies when you bear the unbearable. And it is only in that dark night of the soul that you are prepared to see as God sees and to love as God loves."

—RAM DASS

Reserve some mercy for yourself, so when you are sure that all is lost, there will be one last great power to embrace you.

Surrender

Sometimes others turn from my pain. I hear them offering to help, but I see them slipping away in another direction, afraid to stand by me in such a terrifying place.

It is then that I must preciously guard my own process, and find my way not based on another's estimation, but chosen for my own comfort's sake.

"Everything will be all right."
I awoke one morning to discover that never again would that be true. Hope, it turns out, becomes an obstacle when it keeps us from claiming the present, despairing moment.

Becoming hopeful doesn't mean getting back to the place I used to be in, when "everything is all right." Hope is finding an occasion for joy among the moments of sorrow. Hope is active, affirming the possibility that healing has already begun.

The rational mind is not capable of truly understanding this loss; only the heart has a chance to accept and transform this suffering. For it is not the mind that has been dealt this blow, it is the heart, and it is only there that healing is possible.

The heart, where the entirety of my experience resides in memory and imagination, in the deepest recesses of my soul. It is there I will look for a way out of this hell.

I've heard it said that scar tissue is the strongest stuff of the body. And that when a bone is broken, it grows back stronger than before. If that is true, that I am strongest in my broken places, then the next part of my life will be different indeed.

Come grieve with me, my faithful friend. This is my time for mourning.

When it becomes your time, you also will not be one, but two. We will do it together.

I remember when the sounds of night were stillness or pleasure and a contented sigh. Now each breath utters sounds of struggle as memories of love are exhaled, filling up my breathing space with their persistent images until I must draw them in again, gasping, gulping the ghost-ridden air.

I do not yet understand the necessity of my labored breathing. I do not yet recognize this night song and its healing rhythm.

There is much to trust in grieving. But not because you need put faith in great difficulty. Pain also arouses deep passion and ignites clear understanding within you—strong defenses already in place. Eventually, you will feel confident enough to befriend even the most frightening of feelings.

" Try to raise up the sunken feelings of this enormous past; your personality will grow stronger, your solitude will expand and become a place where you can live in the twilight, where the noise of other people passes by, far in the distance."

—RAINER MARIA RILKE

Mourning is more than recovering from death, it is recovering life. We chase after solace, resolution—an end to the pain. There is nothing to chase after. To find life again, we need only go back to ourselves.

I turned to an old friend, searching for the magic words that would bring me peace. Her answer was silence. There were no words to make it all right; I had been foolish to expect them. The only magic was her great love for me.

I have felt that you were my reason for living. Perhaps I was wrong to give you that much power.

I have to find a new reason for living, meaning that comes from my reclaimed self, power that radiates from my emerging wholeness.

In this way, I will have learned the sweet lesson of letting go.

*G*rief is the process of exhuming all that has been, examining its precious contents, and lovingly preparing it for re-burial.

*S*he grasped my hands tightly, staring into my eyes, past the tears, both hers and mine, into the struggle of my understanding.

"I'll cry with you," she whispered, "until we run out of tears. Even if it's forever. We'll do it together."

There it was . . . a simple promise of connection. The loving alliance of grief and hope that blesses both our breaking apart and our coming together again.

Where once the scar left by death was a painful reminder of lost love, that same love will someday claim the power to transform that scar into a permanent remembrance of joy.

Surrender

After days of wandering in the uncertain pain of my grief, of hiding from my fear, of begging to be brought back safely, I have finally come home to face the occasion of my wandering, and to dwell again in the certainty and safety of myself.

You, my friend, have struggled as I have grieved. Can I relieve you of any doubt? You are doing exactly the right thing. Every time you see me, you allow me to be sad. You say, "It's okay to fall apart. It's more than okay, it's expected."

"God gives us memory so that we may have roses in December."

—JAMES MATTHEW BARRIE

Grief is cruel, stripping us of our defenses,
getting our attention through the shock.
How surprising then, the aftermath of the attack.
The shock becomes focus; the vulnerability, a
purification. Defeat is followed by a victory: the
lasting gift of re-ordering one's life.

Impossible as it may sometimes seem, we survive by remembering. Naturally, we run from the memories that haunt us and the ghosts that hunt us down in our hiding places. Eventually, weariness overtakes us, and there is nothing left to do but face the past.

This is the moment when the curse becomes the blessing. This is the moment when remembering becomes a transforming grace.

The sounds of grief are mysterious. First, the utter stillness. And then, after endless moments of silence, a thunderclap of blessed noisiness may well sound.

For the first time in months, I am alert. I begin to discern sounds I had forgotten . . . curiosity, explanation, argument, conversation, and something suspiciously like laughter.

He was sick so long I couldn't remember when he wasn't. We adjusted, though. We made our daily routine into a song. Hospital visits turned into picnics. We made lists of everything we could still do and we did them all.

Because it was often helpful, we listened to others who had walked the same rutted path. But we planted our own flowers along the way.

I will always remember the times of delight, even as our days together were ending.

The ritual of grieving contains a mysterious and strange song of liberation: Do not forget, do not forget. I would have thought to banish all memories, yet healing demands we include them in the final celebration.

Grieving with someone else acts like a mirror, showing us who and where we are. And you, my friend, have held up the glass for both of us.

And I have seen you changed by my suffering, a reflection of my own transformation. It helps me to see that I am accompanied in my grief; I find strength in the image of our togetherness.

hy is it amid this terrible sadness and missing I feel a strength, a potency I have never felt before? Is it because I have survived my own fear? It is more than that. I faced my most shattered, most vulnerable self, and instead of giving up, I thought to let go.

The first time a memory slides over us like a wave of warmth, we have turned the corner on our grief. When a once painful reminder evokes a gentle laugh, when we recognize the joy of the present in an image from the past, we have arrived at an important moment. Those memories are being transformed, unmistakably, into messages of hope.

*I*f I am to wear this mourning cloak, let it be made of the fabric of love, woven by the fine thread of memory.

Surrender

This storm of grief is inevitable. I find myself caught in its front, threatened from all sides, unsure of my chances. While it rages, I can only hold fast to warm remembrance, to the whispered assurances of a few faithful companions, to the unexpected courage that flows within me. And out of the torrent, my spirit finds safe passage.

What frightens us about grief is its familiarity. Whatever unspeakable pain I am feeling, those around me will also feel someday. I must hold for others the consolation of my shared grief, to be given away again and again as the seasons of mercy and compassion carry us all through our common human experience.

"What is left—or lost—is not a relationship or a place or even a context. What is left is a consciousness that once felt secure, had categories to fit things into, and knew who it was, where it was going, and why. And what replaces this sureness is 'not knowing.' And openness. And something unspeakably, and sometimes almost unbearably, new."

—SHERRY ANDERSON AND
PATRICIA HOPKINS,
The Feminine Face of God

G rieving has made me more than I would have been without it. Of course, I would never have chosen this relentless roller coaster of pain and introspection, but since it chose me, I cannot help but notice the fresh flow of freedom. I have taken up with unexpected new powers.

Today I wake with a slight smile that heralds the hesitant return of pleasure. What did not seem possible only recently may be just around the corner.

TRANSFORMATION

"Everything in life that we really accept
undergoes a change. So suffering must
become Love. That is the mystery."

—KATHERINE MANSFIELD

Surprisingly enough, we are more than sorrow. We are breath and beating heart, we are spirit resilient and possibilities simply unexplored.

What is it I am afraid of? Is it that I myself might be swept away, as easily and as swiftly as my loved ones have been? Or is it what death has reminded me, that I am but a player in his daily game of hide and seek?

We must choose only the game of life, knowing that dying is a mere instant of our living, and not to be what keeps us from exchanging fear for freedom.

"*M*ourning is the constant reawakening that things are now different."

—STEPHANIE ERICSSON

G rief is like a leaky faucet. Just when you think it's fixed, it comes back again, more bothersome than ever.

Perhaps we should not expect an end to the dripping of the faucet or of our tears: there will always be more where they came from. Instead, we can accept the comfort of a rhythmic letting go, knowing each droplet of grief has the potential to cleanse, to soothe, indeed, to nourish new life.

No, this was not "meant to be" and it is certainly not "better this way." How can a death ever be prescribed? How can the loss of hope be better than its fulfillment?

This only is meant to be: the tenderness and fidelity with which we remember the dead and endeavor to fulfill the hopes of the living.

The paradox of healing is that it is both holding on and letting go. We hold onto memories, and we let them go; we hold onto feelings, and we let them go. We hold onto an old way of being, because the self we still are resides there, and we let go to a new way of being, so that the self can live on.

The daily ritual of grieving has dictated my going over and over the details of death. As I slowly heal, the ritual is being transformed. I am beginning to enjoy once again the daily details of life.

*E*very song I hear on the radio I turn into your song. I cry at stoplights and at the beginning and ending of every day. Yet each cleansing tear moves me closer to hearing something I never noticed before—hidden, healing lyrics in the melodies of old and cherished loves.

*T*his season of mourning, like spring,
summer, fall, and winter, will also pass.

"Cancer is not God's will. The death of a child is not God's will. . . deaths from automobile accidents. . . are not God's will. I would rather have no God at all than that kind of punitive God. Tragedies are consequences of human actions, and the only God worth believing in does not cause the tragedies but lovingly comes into the anguish with us."

—MADELINE L 'ENGLE,
Two-Part Invention

The truth that transcends our deepest sorrows is not the good that comes from the bad things that happen, but the good that continues, and even is revealed, despite them.

What does it mean to accept spiritual responsibility for our lives? Somehow, I think this has everything to do with grieving, with recognizing the connectedness of death and life, and of allowing ourselves to be inspired by the mystical power of letting go.

I long to understand it all, but for now I celebrate mere findings.

I hear myself thinking, in a small voice that whispers the unthinkable: "It's okay that you died."

Such a message leaves me troubled. I had thought that after months of fighting with fate and God and medicine, I must have let down my guard long enough for death to sneak in and take you away.

Or did something else happen? Did I stop to catch my breath and while I was simply breathing, you said goodbye and took your leave of me?

That same small voice within continues to nudge me along: "It's okay that you died, and that I am still alive."

What are the words of letting go? If we could manage one more little talk, it would be a loving conversation of echoes, called out through the universe:

Goodbye,
  goodbye.
I forgive you,
    forgive you.
I'll miss you,
      never forget you.
I love you,
        love you, too. . .

Sometimes, thinking of death, feelings of panic would press into my awareness and send me shuddering into myself. But I am calmer now about dying; perhaps I will never be that afraid again. After all, I watched you go away with death and I know that you are all right. I will also go away, and I, too, will be all right.

I worried that all of this suffering was a punishment.

But your death was not a result of misdeeds, yours or mine, some cosmic retaliation for selfishness. It is so very true that bad things happen to good people, just because they happen. Trying to lay blame is a worthless pursuit, and a dangerous one, as it squanders precious energy needed for the task at hand—holding fast to myself and to my own uninterrupted goodness, despite tragedy, despite regret.

The beach house. . .
was designed so that in a bad storm
   the ocean could have a way
      to rush through it
      without doing any major damage. . .
   its beauty is in its durability
and its durability comes
not from offering resistance to the power
   of the ocean
but in finding a way for the water to pass
   through
   thereby saving it
   and letting it stand strong."

—MARTHA MANNING,
A Season of Mercy

To love is to risk losing. To lose is to risk finding something new. The cycle of the heart: birth, death, rebirth. Therefore, before my heart turns to stone, I will re-enter the cycle, and make up my mind again to risk living.

What is it that I have left to do with you?

I must gather up our memories and divide them into two boxes.

In the first I will lovingly set all those things that are gone and can never be replaced. These are the secret signs of our unique understanding. I will mourn these lost treasures as I have mourned you, and then I will give the box away.

In the other I will collect all those things that remain to be shared again in another time and place. Each of these joys you have left to me, with a blessing, to be recreated with other, yet undiscovered loves. I will celebrate these gifts as I have celebrated you, and then this box, I will keep.

" Courage is not the absence of fear and pain, but the affirmation of life despite fear and pain."

—RABBI EARL GROLLMAN

Even as I bow to dismal realities, I listen for an explanation. Even as time leads me toward resignation, my heart longs for understanding.

Will I ever give up my relentless need to know? Only when I become as calm and undaunted as a prophet, only when I become present to the Spirit of Truth, will I find answers or learn to ask different questions.

The path through grief is littered with anger and guilt, emptiness and despair. But there among these roadside heartaches, hiding beneath the dull, dead weeds that have so entangled our spirits, are tiny possibilities for laughter. Each day they grow stronger, and soon they will burst forth and flourish, until the remnants of our pain are covered with their colors.

Death, with its power of separation, sometimes tempts us to remain alone. We resist by doing what death least expects—daring to love, reaching out to still another human being.

While grief enters the house as a stranger, it often leaves as a friend. A messenger who brings unwanted news, grief stays to endure our disbelief and to encourage us to step outside again, where the air is fresh with acceptance.

I am fighting the temptation to plot revenge.

From within my torment, a very loud voice drowns out what is left of my humanity: "Even the score!"

Frantically, I argue. Retribution will not bring you back, I say. What I choose to do in your memory will be your legacy and my reason to go on.

Beneath the din, another, softer voice—perhaps my old self—quietly states my position. . . . In your name, I want to live to celebrate the last act of inhumanity.

I feel that I could protect myself from further grief by dealing only with things that cannot change. But that would separate me from surprise. To no longer be delighted by a revelation or a capricious moment of love—that is too high a price to pay for keeping me from unknown, yet certain, sorrows.

The mystery of death is not so different from the mystery of life. Life calls forth transformation to sanctify it, and death calls forth transformation to redeem it. In that paradox is the promise of holiness.

*I*n an inconsolable experience, we ought to get huge quantities of wisdom and grace.

There is the chance to see our pain from God's point of view: Human creatures getting recklessly involved in caring about one another and discovering in the process the infinite, indestructible power of love.

All of these good things are available to us at the very high price of letting go.

" *I* do not want ever to be indifferent to the joys and beauties of this life. For through these, as through pain, we are enabled to see purpose in randomness, pattern in chaos. We do not have to understand in order to believe that behind the mystery and the fascination there is love."

—MADELINE L 'ENGLE,
Two-Part Invention

Healing is about taking what you need and then leaving the pain place. What is the moment of departure from the pain? It is knowing what needs were being met by the lost relationship and choosing to have them met in other ways.

At the moment I begin to meet on my own the needs left wanting by loss, I move away from my pain, and toward the place of transformation.

We cannot avoid change, nor can we protect ourselves from it. We can only accept the inevitable—that things will change—and decide to embrace the categories of large and small rather than bad and good.

The world is dangerous. At every corner, separation and sadness await our crossing, sabotaging our happiness and stealing our hope.

Knowing this, we risk living anyway, we risk loving anyway. And the pain and loss that comes is not given to us as a personal test, but simply as a consequence of being alive.

How could this be? After struggling with my anger, my utter aloneness, my sadness bordering on despair, I am left with . . . a sense of freedom? Having survived the unthinkable, I am not as afraid of the ways of destiny, nor as unfamiliar with the capriciousness of change. Whatever will happen to me next . . . will happen to me next.

ife will not go on in the same way without him. If it were the same, we could only conclude his life meant nothing, made no contribution. The fact that he left behind a place that cannot be filled is a high tribute to the uniqueness of his soul.

Just as an emerging creature must let go of the place from where it came and push forward to something new, we too must abandon the darkness, which by now has become consoling and safe, and reluctantly re-enter, wrestling and weeping, the world to which we have been assigned responsibility and residence.

*I*t would seem that the cycle of life begins not with birth, but rebirth. The newness of spring buds, or babies, or facets of a relationship, comes not from something that wasn't there before, but from some old miracle of love that delights in change.

Death cannot create an ending without a remnant from which the new can grow. Death, like birth and rebirth, is simply on its way around, over and over again.

When order and understanding are shot to hell by loss, we might assume that it is chance and not any effort on our part that governs the world.

But it is not chance that defines our lives but change, and that is, perhaps, something we can learn to live with.

And when I find myself bemoaning the intransigence of it all, I might start examining the possibility of transforming it all.

" *I* cannot cause light, the most I can do is try to put myself in the path of its beam...

"It is possible, in deep space, to sail on solar wind. Light, be it particle or wave, has force: you rig a giant sail and go. The secret of seeing is to sail on solar wind. Hone and spread your spirit till you yourself are a sail, whetted, translucent, broadside to the nearest puff."

—ANNIE DILLARD

inally one night it happened. We came together once more in a dream to say goodbye. It was something that had been left out, and for a long time I had searched for a better ending.

It was so much more than a goodbye. It was many things at once, memories and stories and celebration. And when it was time to part, it was hardly an ending, but a blessing, really, of everything we continue to be to each other.

Perhaps there will be another dream someday. And our conversation will continue, without a beginning or an end, as it is with love.

CONTINUANCE

"In the beginning everything was in relationship,
and in the end everything will be in relationship
again. In the meantime, we live by hope."

—JEAN LANIER

The joyous creation of a time and space shared in love is both delicate and indestructible. Death clumsily ransacks this holy place where two people have loved, but can never reach their inner sanctum.

Rest assured that in her dying, in her flight through darkness toward a new light, she held you in her arms and carried your closeness with her. And when she arrived at God, your image was imprinted on her joy-filled soul.

What is immutable is love and its sheer power. Not even death can diminish its possibilities.

When one lives and the other dies, the survivor is not guilty of snatching up what will make life continue for himself, but only of being in the presence of life's ending for another.

Continuing to live is not a sin. It is a fortunate necessity.

There is a deep ache in my arms. They throb with loneliness, for the feel of you next to me, the way the space closed so tightly between us, signifying our eagerness to be, for a moment, one.

What I miss the most is knowing the joyful presence of love in an embrace; my arms will always reach for you, at least in sweet memory.

Continuance

We noticed every minute we were with him, saying to ourselves, "remember this time." Now that he is gone, we rejoice in our wisdom and in our deliberate memories.

Sometimes, rarely, it happens that way; we prepare for a loss by cherishing a presence. But when left unprepared, presence is still possible, if we recognize its transformation into memories, not as deliberate this time, but precious nonetheless.

The ghosts of regret did not return today to mark the anniversary of your death. This time, there was no struggle to hide from memory and imagination. Where once I braced for a backward slide into confusion and guilt, I now prepared to celebrate the years of our mystical companionship.

So when you were there to greet me at dawn, your presence was warmly welcomed. Together, we ushered in the day.

Continuance

*I*n life's experience, the closest thing to dying might be the act of giving birth. The moment of letting go and giving forth is one of utter freedom and contentment. How close it is to the moment of letting go and moving on, of innocent liberation and well-deserved calm. These are extraordinary moments, mystically linked to every other birthing, and dying, in the universe.

It is comforting to believe that the occasions of greatest transformation spring from the same source—surely another hint of something more, something greater, than ourselves.

" The world is a quiet place . . . its images forever fixed. They do not vanish. They can be remembered, and they can be foreseen. Nothing and no one are lost."

—MARK HELPRIN,
A Soldier of the Great War

No one can ever take your place."

Perhaps I was hasty when I first said that, and confused all of the times I've said it since.

I will carry you with me only as far as I allow myself to be changed by your love. I will grow from my memories of you when I invite someone else to enter my life and begin to fill up the space you once filled.

eath bequeaths us endings that appear to be certain. Only love proposes another legacy, the inheritance of hope just as absolute.

Continuance

Where are you? I have been searching for your continuation beyond the boundaries of my small space. I have wanted to believe you still exist somewhere else. Somewhere separate, but near to me.

I need only to look inside. I will find you there, shining steady at the end of a silver thread of love that will connect us forever to the most powerful truth that has ever been or ever will be.

What do we do with the leftovers of our love?
His telephone number was so familiar
that I could play it, like a one-handed melody on
the piano. To ease that intimate motion out of the
repertoire of daily life is so painful, but I do it
knowing that the eternal grace of our friendship
does not depend on the memory of a motion, but
on the magic of our conversation.

Continuance

We put all of our energy into a relationship, and even with its ups and down, its anguish and its ecstasy, what comes out is something of a miracle.

With the loss of a love we are tempted to believe we expended all that energy, so rich with love and creativity, for nothing. We must resist, for every miracle is as timeless and limitless as Eternity.

Mourning is tuning into the you who is still here, despite death.

People speak of you less often now. The things you did are being done by others. I no longer notice your lingering presence in every room.

Then an old friend calls and we tell forgotten tales, or I find a place of yours not yet emptied by my grieving. And I am touched by the reality of you once more, and quietly I celebrate your continuance.

I started missing you long before you were gone. I'll keep loving you long after the memories bring you back.

Resurrection. The reversal of what was thought to be absolute. The turning of midnight into dawn, hatred into love, dying into living anew.

But if we look closely into life, we will find that resurrection is more than hope; it is our experience. The return to life from death is something we understand at our innermost depths, something we feel on the surface of our tender skin. We have come back to life, not only when we start to shake off the shroud of sorrow that has bound us, but when we begin to believe in all that is still endlessly possible.

Extraordinary things do happen in the ordinary moments of our lives, and in those times when nothing less than a miracle is needed.

I come closer to the presence of the Eternal
in the depth of my grief over losing you,
the power of the passion I still feel for you, the
endlessness of my belief in who you are, and
the wisdom I possess to know that all of this will
always be true.

Continuance

They wonder where the part of me that was you has gone. "Part of her died, too," they say.

They don't understand. Even now, we are side by side. That doesn't mean that I can't go on living without you. It just means that I will believe in you every day of my life.

" Be joyful though you have considered all the facts."

—WENDELL BERRY

Continuance

Somehow your departing song is both sad and wonderful, a melody to dance to, to sing, to bring me to tears. I cannot help this; your dying, like existence itself, has a life of its own. As sad as I am, I cannot help but hum along.

People who are still alive cannot simply be exchanged for the one who has died. Each love comes to us uniquely.

Therefore, we can not replace what we have lost with a similar affection. And we need not report to anyone the pure pleasure of a new love.

I look to the stars and I see you there.

It may seem that all that can be known of your life is a quick flash, just a small part of the excitement and the confusion, the certainty and the doubt that once was you.

But I know more. I know the bravest part of you, the part that risked loving. So when I look up to see you, I have no doubt that at least your courage will shine forever.

safe passage

In a dream I walked with the Divine through the wondrous expanse of creation, past every sweet stirring of life and into an infinity that breathed as I breathe, setting the tiny alongside the magnificent, sparkling and shimmering in delight of its own oneness. And there, snug between the splendid spirits of every earthly love, was you.

Continuance

How could this be? I have mourned your loss for many days, many months. I have wondered if I could ever live again. But now I know your death has made me more alive.

That I would survive is amazing. That I would live more fully is unexplainable.

You are not lost. You continue in every hearty laugh, in every nice surprise, and in every reassuring moment of my life.

Continuance

Now that he is gone, never hesitate to tell his story. He has left you behind with treasures to be shared. When you remember, your memories are sent far into the future, a sweet heritage for all those who will come after. And be assured that your story is being told, too, somewhere, to a rapt audience of all those who came before.

When I miss you, I can talk to that part of me that is you.

If I am quiet and begin to listen for the you inside of me, your voice will urge me into gentle conversation.

We will speak of never really being alone.

Continuance

I can do something marvelous with my grief. Despite everything that has happened, despite even death, I can still love you, and I will still love others.

" I have a friend who is an artist. Before he left Vietnam forty years ago, his mother held his hand and told him, 'Whenever you miss me, look into your hand, and you will see me immediately.'

"The presence of his mother is not just genetic. Her spirit, her hopes, and her life are also in him. When he looks into his hand, he can see thousands of generations before him and thousands of generations after him. . . . He told me that he never feels lonely."

—THICH NHAT HANH,
Peace is Every Step

Continuance

I can look into the world and see you in every act of love. Where once you were one, you are now many.

safe passage

Although you are no longer here to safeguard them, the things that you brought into the world—integrity and gladness and your capacity for love—can never be driven out. I will make sure of that.

Continuance

Today I visited a holy place. I stood there on the shore, smiling, aware of you in every swooping gull, in every bead of moisture that arose from the foaming surf. It is here that we finally understood love's power, and thus made this place holy by our very presence. It is where we said, "There must be a God, because I am loved by you."

have sensed your presence so often I no longer need to search for you. I can relax and go about my life, leaving that sorry task for those who still worry about forgetting, or being forgotten.

hank you for being part of my life. It is time to move on. I bow inwardly to the memory of you and, turning away, stand straight to face the new day.

Grieve as God grieves, trembling over the power of the love that seems lost, but is only changing.

Living through the dying of someone close to me is different than anything I have ever imagined. The dark cloud of unknowing that once cast long shadows on any sense of understanding is gone. Instead, we are somehow inside of death, the two of us, and we find that we are able to begin or end, to remain or move on.

" I suddenly knew that all souls who ever lived left some shape or energy or impression that continued to inhabit the earth out of reach of ordinary consciousness. . . . I was only sure that I was propelled through the veil of unknowing to the other side where everything is bathed in light."

—EDWARD TICK

"Her spirit will always be with you," they told me, over and over again. And on some days, yes, I can feel it.

But don't they know that my spirit is with her, too. I could feel me leaving with her. We had paused at death's door, and when it was time, we turned and smiled at each other, ready for a new adventure. Arms linked, our step jaunty, we moved easily down some long lighted corridor of blessed passing. I was there, at her side, while something was ending and something else was beginning.

And that same spirit of mine, some small trace of me, is with her now, in her new place. Yes, I can feel it. I can feel it.

To be joyful in the universe is a brave and reckless act. The courage for joy springs not from the certainty of human experience, but the surprise. Our astonishment at being loved, our bold willingness to love in return—these wonders promise the possibility of joyfulness, no matter how often and how harshly love seems to be lost.

CONNECTION

"Death by itself may not encourage connections.
It may simply drive home more deeply the solitude
of loss. But love encourages, and even builds,
connections, and there is no way to
separate love and death."

—ROBERT MCAFEE BROWN

$\mathcal{E}$ mpathy is the alchemy of grief's experience. We first make room for ourselves in a heart crowded with memories and regret, offering a gentle welcome and a safe place to mourn. We then turn to the others who wait outside, and in comprehending their heartache, we ask them to dwell also within our hearts. In this way, we ourselves are healed.

When we grieve, we are unwittingly linked to a profound power that is as termless as time and as common as human experience. We have seen evidence of that power in places made holy by the poor and oppressed, who despite their untold suffering still find occasions for joy, who despite the constancy of their mourning still find reasons to believe. Indeed, this is a mystical force, waiting to honor each of us, in our grieving times.

" Pray that your loneliness may spur you into finding something to live for, great enough to die for."

—DAG HAMMARSKJOLD

Connection

In a quiet moment, I reflect that my sorrow is as familiar as it is mysterious. I consider the chance that what is happening to me is sudden, complete awareness of an ongoing human event. I imagine grief to be a universal truth, not beginning with me, but beginning in the grand expanse of time and space and finding me when my turn has come.

We should never doubt the potency of compassion. When the torment of one person leads another deeper into her own experience, all of humanity has taken one marvelous step forward. The magic of this moment is breathtaking: a human being has chosen to be moved, and changed, by the distress of someone other than himself.

A song of lamentation is best sung by many.
From within that ensemble arises the sound
of mourning that is no longer lonely—rich,
healing, harmonies that dare to accompany the
harsh discordance of the world.

llowing someone else's anguish to break our hearts is as surprising as falling in love. The world is turned upside down. We are drawn to her side; being with him is a holy experience.

In places where misery is the stuff of life, they call it solidarity. It is grieving for the world because of the death of one child. It is responding to suffering by making it our own.

In these same places, it is said that new life is birthed as constantly as the dead are buried. Everyone who becomes part of this very deep dying also becomes part of a very deep rising.

"If we can say that grace is a sense of connectedness, that it is the experience of our underlying nature, then we may see how what is often called tragedy holds the seeds of grace. We see that what brings us to grace is not always pleasant, though it seems always to take us to something essential in ourselves."

—STEPHEN LEVINE,
Who Dies?

When you truly enter into your sadness, you come to a precious moment of understanding of the absolute value of the life of one human being. And if you can hold to the meaning of one life and one death, you will come to the meaning of all existence.

The pearl inside your cavern of grief is this instant of knowing, and after your mourning time, you will remember what you have learned, and never allow a single life to be devalued again.

Connection

O ut of ignorance, or perhaps fear, it has been said about the people of the Third World: "It is different for them. They're used to people dying."

Anyone who has grieved understands the inhumanity of those words. As if familiarity with loss, often violent and unspeakable, makes it easier. They are not "used to" death. They have, however, come to recognize the constant prod of anger and loneliness; they know intimately the dark chamber of despair. A tortured spirit might be dulled into submission, but never acceptance.

Although the experience of loss has infinite variations, in the darkness the voices that cry out at the final moment of separation are indistinguishable. Alongside the one goodbye we recognize so well, so many others can be heard, a chorus of parting that is happening all over the world.

Grief brings the unexpected. Lost relationships are recovered, loving friendships are renewed. In each other's pain we acknowledge our own fragile humanity; we recognize the desperate fight of another against death and its unthinkable claims. The connection is spellbinding, calling us out into the universe when we are ready.

" You can hold back the suffering of the world, you have free permission to do so and it is in accordance with your nature, but perhaps this very holding back is the one suffering you could have avoided."

—FRANZ KAFKA

A woman in El Salvador who lost two sons to the guns of the death squads stands vigil in front of military headquarters every day. She is not afraid. "They have taken everything from me. Why should I fear death?"

Others come to stand beside her. Her grief has set her free, and her freedom empowers those who still have everything to lose. To the forces of death, they raise voices fueled by the forces of love.

To be spiritual is to feel deeply. It is entering the world of emotion and humanity. For what makes us most human is not that we reason correctly, but that we feel uncontrollably.

Other creatures organize experience in a way that helps them survive. But human beings live in emotions that make complex the inner self, and invite them into spiritual empathy with all of life.

Connection

What we share with others who mourn is something we would rather not, yet it allows us to be seers in a sightless world. When we dare to examine images of evil and inhumanity, we are left insisting that compassion is the ultimate empowerment. That bond of love, in possession of our weary hearts, can make of us a legion of resistance to the unnecessary suffering of many.

I imagine a place, not far away, where grief is experienced with staggering repetition. There is no horizon, no sun, nothing ahead but death.

It is to this place that we might bring our own new source of healing light. The steady glow that comes from each inner fire will rise together until one cannot be distinguished from another. Where one ends the other begins, until all is light.

Connection

Because my pain begins to resemble that which is felt by so many others, and because my hurt escapes my singular experience and joins a whole universe of anguish, then to my great surprise, I claim some small role in the story—yet to be told—of humanity's survival.

For any of us who believe in the continued presence of love in a world yearning for kindness, our shared vulnerability, the echo of our grieving, and our common trepidation about the future become a spiritual event.

It is this sacred trembling that acknowledges the reality of the suffering world. Our cosmic, quaking fear for the children of this planet is as sure as the tragedy that continues to befall them.

The task at hand is to translate fear into wisdom, and wisdom into the laughter of future generations.

Connection

What exists, sometimes, in places where grief and its powers have visited many times, is compassion more fully realized. Where vision is not blurred by detachment, the sorrowing see clearly the causes of their affliction. Where hope is no longer tomorrow's promise of consolation, they choose to believe in today's cry of protest. In the mirror image of their concern, love is transformed into resistance.

Healing is always a propulsion toward others, not an abandoning of the most valuable healer—the self—but an expansion of that new self into the world, bearing the lessons it has learned.

"Despair cannot be banished by injections of optimism or sermons on 'positive thinking.' Like grief, it must be acknowledged and worked through. This means it must be named and validated as a healthy, normal human response to the situation we find ourselves in. Faced and experienced, its power can be used, as the frozen defenses of the psyche thaw and new energies are released."

—JOANNA MACY,
World as Lover, World as Self

*E*mpowerment comes to those who move aside their own desolation to make room for that of another.

It is true. From within the entangled arms of the grieving, a new energy is unleashed, something enormous and untapped. What finally breaks free of that embrace is a ferocious love, and a courage so boundless that it defies even death and those who have become death's agents.

Comforting one another, we will come to know this power.

Connection

*I*f you share my tears, if you take the first merciful step toward me, if you walk bravely into what I am feeling, then we begin to bring down the power of despair.

The march of the grieving is both desperate and defiant. Each step taken together gives meaning to what appeared to be meaningless. Each brush of shoulder to shoulder closes the gap between separation and solidarity. Whatever happens, from this moment on, will be grounded in a sacred partnership.

Connection

Of all of the powers bestowed on the grieving, the most mystifying is being able to see in the dark. And of all the secrets of the universe that are only visible at blackest night, the most holy is the power of compassion.

The heavens send a message to all those who grieve: Rather than being consumed by sorrow, could it be that you are becoming fire?

Make of your grief first glowing ember, then wildfire, and bring your burning hope to another.

Make of your grief wildfire—the wisdom of your experience will ignite the passion of your joining.

"No one is as capable of gratitude as one who has emerged from the kingdom of night. We know that every moment is a moment of grace, every hour an offering; not to share them would mean to betray them. Our lives no longer belong to us alone; they belong to all those who need us desperately."

—ELIE WIESEL

Allow your woundedness to send you into the world rather than withdraw from it. Allow the wisdom of your solemn experience to inform your heart and send you racing to the side of the suffering.

INDEX